POWER FOR TODAY

MARTY FOLEY

xulon
PRESS

Copyright © 2015 by Marty Foley

Power For Today
by Marty Foley

Printed in the United States of America.

ISBN 9781498433792

All rights reserved solely by the author. The author guarantees all contents are original and do not infringe upon the legal rights of any other person or work. No part of this book may be reproduced in any form without the permission of the author. The views expressed in this book are not necessarily those of the publisher.

Unless otherwise indicated, Scripture quotations taken from the King James Version (KJV) – *public domain.*

All Hebrew or Greek definitions or references are drawn from the STRONGS EXHAUSTIVE CONCORDANCE OF THE BIBLE.

www.xulonpress.com

Introduction

POWER. What do you think of when you hear the word? Countless wars have been fought to gain it. Vast fortunes have been spent to attain it. Why are people so desperate to possess it? What is so important about it?

In this age, people are all about having power. Many accumulate great school bills as they pursue an education that will empower them to accomplish career goals. An entire segment of our economy has been built upon people exercising and working out in an effort to gain strength, power.

Every realm of our existence requires power in some respect. This is especially true with regard to the spiritual realm. Since the moment of the first 'power grab' attempted by Lucifer in the Heavenlies, there has been an ongoing struggle for power. Lucifer wants the power to destroy mankind. Men need the power of God to resist him. And there is a constant battle going on to prevent people from ever truly learning of and experiencing the very Power that Heaven has ordained for them.

The devil, Satan, doesn't want people to know that there is available to them power, strength and ability to be and do all that God has called us to. Yet the Truth remains the same. There is hope. There is help. There is Power for you to live an obedient, overcoming, victorious life in Jesus Christ.

This book is written in the hope that all that read it will awaken to that which Heaven has provided for them. That they will arise and pursue the Promise that has been offered to them. And that they will encounter and experience for themselves the greatness of the Power that God desires to fill their lives with. If we've ever needed it, the time is now.

THERE IS POWER FOR TODAY!

Chapter 1 – POWER

Acts 1:8
"But ye shall receive power, after that the Holy Ghost is come upon you: and ye shall be witnesses…"

The Bible makes it clear that God's Plan is for His people to be victorious in overcoming sin. God's people are to be witnesses to a lost and dying world. To ensure that they are, He has provided POWER from Heaven. Unfortunately, it seems that far too many today are unfamiliar with this Power that is available to them. They do not know what is theirs for the having.

Knowledge is a critical component of our existence. With it, survival is not merely possible, it is probable. But the lack of knowledge has more than once led to people's destruction.

Hosea 4:6
"My people are destroyed for lack of knowledge."

Accepting and acting upon accurate information is key to our well being and success.

John 8:32
"And ye shall know the truth, and the truth shall make you free."

For Christians, followers of Jesus Christ, the Truth is the written Word of God, the Holy Bible. It is the revelation of teachings and principles that God has provided for us. While Jesus ministered as a man, He gave many truths and teachings that have been captured for us to study, to apply to our lives and pass on to all that will receive from us.

But when it came to the last few moments of His time upon Earth with His disciples, Jesus did not tell His disciples to remember all that He had taught them. The focus wasn't upon knowledge. Instead,

Chapter 1 – Power

Jesus told them that they were going to receive Power from Heaven into their lives.

Let's take a moment to reflect upon some facts the Bible provides us concerning Jesus, the man, as a minister of the Kingdom of God.

Luke 4:1-13 provides the story concerning Jesus' season of being tempted by the devil. Then we move to the next verse of this chapter.

Luke 4:14
"And Jesus returned in the power of the Spirit into Galilee: and there went out the fame of him through all the region."

From the beginning of His ministry as a servant of the Kingdom of God, Jesus did so in the power of the Holy Spirit.

Next we turn to the Book of Acts for insight on this subject.

Acts 10:38
"How God anointed Jesus of Nazareth with the Holy Ghost and with power: who went

about doing good, and healing all that were oppressed of the devil: for God was with him."

I suspect that many fail to grasp the importance of the information this scripture provides us. In the New Testament, when the Lord Jesus is referred to as Jesus of Nazareth, it is to be understood as a reference to His humanity. So when we read this verse, we are to understand that the writer was speaking of Jesus as a man and of how this man was anointed with the Holy Ghost and power.

When Jesus stepped onto the stage of public ministry, He did not do so under the authority of or with the power of His Sonship to the Almighty God.

Philippians 2:7
"But made himself of no reputation, and took upon him the form of a servant, and was made in the likeness of men."

The Amplified Version Bible's translation of this passage provides us valuable insight as well.

Chapter 1 – Power

> **Philippians 2:7**
> *"But stripped Himself (of all privileges and rightful dignity), so as to assume the guise of a servant (slave), in that He became like men and was born a human being."*

Jesus did not operate by nor perform miracles by virtue of his nature as the Son of God. Jesus is the Son of God. But if He had acted within His own divine power, then no one else could ever hope to do the miraculous things he did, because we do not measure up to His sinlessness. No, he laid aside His divine attributes, His nature and abilities, to function as a flesh and blood man that had been filled and anointed with the Power of the Holy Ghost.

Furthermore, when Jesus came on the scene, He did not do so as merely an anointed teacher of divine truths. Yes, everyone needed to hear the true and accurate information regarding entrance into the Kingdom of Heaven. But the blind and deaf people needed more than information. They needed healing. Individuals being haunted, harassed, and harmed by demonic spirits needed more than well prepared motivational speeches. They needed liberation.

People whose lives are being decimated and destroyed by the devil need more than a "word of encouragement". They need deliverance. And this was what Jesus came to do.

I John 3:8

"For this purpose the Son of God was manifested, that He might destroy the works of the devil."

In the original Greek language, this word that we interpret as "destroy" comes from a root word that means "to loose". That is to say "to break up, to destroy, to dissolve, melt, put off"[1].

Jesus came not merely as a messenger of Heavenly Revelation, but even more so as a minister of earthly liberation. He came not just to tell people about freedom one day in Heaven, but to set them free then and there in the midst of their earthly circumstances. Jesus was manifested to destroy, to tear down and to undo the evil works that Satan was enslaving mankind with.

---

[1] 1:Strong's Exhaustive Concordance Of The Bible

Chapter 1 – Power

Now, at this point, here is where things start to really get exciting for you and me!

John 20:21
"[A]s my Father hath sent me, even so send I you."

Jesus told his disciples, "For the same purpose that my Father sent me forth, now I am sending you forth."

There is no doubt that all mankind stood in need of hearing the Truth that could set them free. But there were many that needed more than just a message of liberation. They needed to encounter ministers that walked in and exercised the Power of liberation. They needed healing, deliverance and restoration.

As a man, Jesus established this kind of active hands-on ministry to the multitudes of people. But then, He laid down His life as the sacrifice for the sins of mankind.

When He took up His life again, He turned this ministry over to His disciples. He said, "As I was sent out, so now I am sending you". Jesus told them that they were going to go out and do the very same things that He had been doing as a witness to the Kingdom of God.

Before Jesus ascended into the clouds, He gave those that were gathered there their next assignment. He told them that they were to go back to their common meeting place and to wait upon the experience of the baptism of the Holy Ghost. He told them that they would receive power.

The word "power" is the same word here in Acts 1:8, as is used in both Luke 4:14 and Acts 10:38. It is an English interpretation of the Greek word dunamis[2]. Perhaps that word sounds vaguely familiar to you. There is good reason for it. That Greek word dunamis is the foundational source from which the modern word dynamite comes from. Most of us know what dynamite is and what it is used for. It is an explosive agent used to destroy and remove objects that are in the path of progress. Mountains standing in the way of roads being constructed have been leveled by the use of dynamite. Locked doors or gates that have kept prisoners captive have been blown off their hinges with the proper application of dynamite.

---

[2] 2:Strong's Exhaustive Concordance Of The Bible

But the dynamite power of Heaven that Jesus spoke of is vastly superior to any earthly dynamite. Man's power or dynamite is only useful to explode and destroy hindrances. Heaven's dunamis does not merely act in a destructive manner.

The power from above not only is capable of releasing the captives but is also able to restore and to revive. The dunamis that Jesus spoke of is Heaven's power not only to drive sickness out of the human body but also has the power to restore health and wellness to their being.

Jesus had ministered in and by the Power of the Holy Spirit. He recognized that this was necessary for His disciples to experience and to operate within themselves. Jesus' disciples were to continue the spiritual war that Jesus had begun against the same devil. They were going to face the same destructive and devastating power of Hell that Jesus had witnessed at work in the world. They didn't just need a mind full of knowledge that they could share with people. They needed a soul full of the Power that opens blinded eyes and sets the captives free. They needed to be filled with the Power of the Holy Spirit.

Upon receiving the Holy Spirit at Pentecost, these disciples immediately began to operate in a greater level of authority and accomplishment than previously experienced. The Scriptures make it evident that they understood the need for this Power and authority to continue to abide and be active in their lives. In Acts chapter four, Peter and John were forcibly brought before the Jewish religious council to give account for having healed a lame man through the name of Jesus. After being threatened by these religious leaders, Peter and John returned to the believers' gathering place and reported their experience.

They then, as a group, lifted their voice to Heaven and called out for God to give them boldness to continue witnessing. And they asked the Lord to continue to demonstrate mighty works, supernatural signs to their audiences. And we are offered this report of what happened:

Acts 4:31
"And when they had prayed, the place was shaken where they were assembled together; and they were all filled with the

Holy Ghost, and they spoke the word of God with boldness."

At this event, it is evident that they had a fresh experience, that is to say another encounter of being "filled with the Holy [Spirit]". Furthermore, we are told that Heaven confirmed the preaching of Jesus with acts of power.

Acts 4:33
"And with great power gave the apostles witness of the resurrection of the Lord Jesus: and great grace was upon them all."

The word power used here, again, comes from the same Greek word dunamis. The disciples had quickly come to understand their dependence upon the Power of God to bear witness to the message they brought.

The world that those disciples faced is the same one that you and I exist in today. The only difference is the following facts; one, we are now closer to the end of the church age than we have ever been, and two, there are more human beings on this planet than in any point past. There are more people that need to be reached with the Gospel witness.

There are more people that can be victims of Satan's attacks and oppression. And there are more people than ever that can be used by the hand of Satan to reject and resist the Message of Life through Jesus Christ.

That is why the witness of the Power of the Gospel of Jesus Christ is so desperately needed. Victims of the attack of Satan do not merely need spiritual hope. They need healing and help. Prisoners of sin do not only need words of deliverance. They need the Power of deliverance to set them free. Weak, helpless people do not need a little pick-me-upper sermonette from Christian messages. They need to be infused with a Power that makes them strong and mighty for the Kingdom of God.

This is the dunamis, the Power of Heaven. This is the Power that was promised to those first disciples. This is the Power that was poured out from Heaven upon them. This is the Power that is still available for needy people like you and I. There is Power for us to not only survive, but to thrive as witnesses for the Kingdom of God. There is Power for Today!

Chapter 2 – THE PROBLEM

Romans 7:15-20

"I do not understand what I do. For what I want to do I do not do, but what I hate I do. And if I do what I do not want to do, I agree that the law is good. As it is, it is no longer I myself who do it, but it is sin living in me. For I know that good itself does not dwell in me, that is, in my sinful nature. For I have the desire to do what is good, but I cannot carry it out. For I do not do the good I want to do, but the evil I do not want to do – this I keep on doing. Now if I do what I do not want to do, it is no longer I who do it, but it is sin living in me that does it."

(New International Version)

In this passage of Scripture, the Apostle Paul dealt with the problem that has haunted Mankind since the fateful moment that Adam and Eve disobeyed the Father's will for them. What is this problem? Here it is in a nutshell. **We may know what is right, but we do not have the ability, the "Power" to do what is right in and of ourselves.**

Mankind does not have, nor can we produce, the ability to be what our Heavenly Father has called us to be and do.

Leviticus 11:45
"[Y]e shall therefore be holy, for I am holy."

I Peter 1:15-16
"But as he which hath called you is holy, so be ye holy in all manner of conversation; because it is written "Be ye Holy; for I AM Holy'."

The first and foremost calling that Christians, disciples of Jesus Christ, have is the calling to a holy lifestyle. Every other calling is subsequent to and dependent upon us making this our highest priority.

Chapter 2 – The Problem

Just how important, how imperative is the issue of holiness?

Hebrews 12:14
"Follow peace with all men, and holiness, without which no man shall see the Lord."

Let us additionally consider the Amplified Version Bible's translation of this verse.

Hebrews 12:14
"Strive to live in peace with everybody and pursue that consecration and holiness without which no one will (ever) see the Lord."

Holiness is an issue of eternal importance. Without holiness in our lives we will not be accepted by God.

Furthermore, Paul saw the problem we all face. He explained it like this: I know what I ought to do, but I fail to do it. And I know what I shouldn't do, yet I find myself doing it anyway! And for people that are supposed to be pursuing a holy lifestyle, that's a real problem.

In the Amplified Version, Paul's words offer us some insight as to what the real cause of this problem was.

Romans 7:18

"For I know that nothing good dwells within me, that is, in my flesh. I can will what is right, but I cannot perform it. (I have the intention and urge to do what is right, but no power to carry it out.)"

In essence, Paul said the problem isn't in knowing the right thing to do or even wanting to do the right thing. The problem is that I do not have the power, the strength, the ability to do those things.

God has called us to be His people. He has called us to be holy. He has called us to be living witnesses of the Kingdom of God. The problem is that we do not have the power, the ability to be all that we have been called to be.

Instead, our lives are occupied by and controlled by the spirit of disobedience.

Chapter 2 – The Problem

> **Ephesians 2:2**
> *"Wherein in the past we walked according to the course of this world, according to the prince of the power of the air, the spirit that now worketh in the children of disobedience."*

The human nature is a fallen, sinful nature. Before the truth of God's liberating power comes into our lives, we are all slaves to sin. When truth enters in, we have the revelation of hope that we can turn from our evil ways. But it takes more than knowing what we ought to do.

Just ask the Apostle Peter. Perhaps you are familiar with what happened to him. The story is found in Matthew, Chapter 26. Peter was a man that loved Jesus deeply. Yet Jesus knew the weakness of Peter's spiritual nature. He forewarned Peter that he was going to find himself denying Jesus in a moment of intense pressure. Peter told Jesus that he would not. Yet when the time came, he did it anyway. Peter knew what he shouldn't do, but he still did it. He knew what he should do, yet he didn't do it. Was Peter an unbeliever? Of course not. Was he a backslider? By no means!

Paul said in Romans 7:18, there was nothing good dwelling in his flesh (his human nature). He had no power to do what was right. Like Paul, Peter was a man. He did not have the Power, the ability to rise to the occasion and be what he needed to be.

This was the problem that plagued Paul and Peter. It is the same problem that has plagued all Mankind down through the ages. It is the same problem that believers face today.

We, the Church, are called to present to the World a living, Power-filled witness of the Love of Jesus Christ. We are called to present the witness of a holy lifestyle before the World. We are called to preach the Word of hope to a hopeless world. We are called to provide the World with miraculous help through healings and deliverance. We are called to stand up and be what Heaven intends us to be.

We know how we are supposed to live. We know what we are supposed to be. I believe that many of us desire to be faithful to our calling. Yet we find ourselves not doing what we ought to do, but in fact doing the opposite. Does this mean we are not believers? I don't think so. Does it mean that we don't love God? I think not. Perhaps it could be, however, that like our forefathers, we have a problem. What is this problem? It is that we, of ourselves, are devoid, empty of the Power that we need to please God. We don't have it "in" us to be pleasing to God. While we desire to do great things for God, in and of ourselves, we cannot.

Deuteronomy 5:27, 29
"Go near and listen to all that the Lord our God says. Then tell us whatever the Lord our God tells you. We will listen and obey."

"Oh, that their hearts would be inclined to fear me and keep my commands always, so that it might go well with them and their children forever!"

The Lord God called the people of Israel to draw near to Him in order to speak personally to them. Their fear caused them to reject this invitation. Instead, they urged Moses to go in their place and come back with God's rules. Their intent was to try to 'live up to' God's requirements. What was God's response to this? He said, 'if only they had a true heart to do this.' I believe that in essence He was saying 'if only they had the ability, the Power, to do this.'

But as a people, neither Old Testament Israel, nor any other peoples of the earth could be what God has called men to be. They couldn't, and we of ourselves can't either, because of the problem we all share.

Thank God we haven't been left with our problem and no hope of a solution!

Ezekiel 11:19-20

"And I will give them one heart, and I will put a new spirit within you: and I will take the stony heart out of their flesh, and will give them a heart of flesh. That they may walk in my statutes, and keep mine ordinances, and do them: and they shall be my people, and I will be their God."

I believe what God was saying was, 'My people have a problem. They need a new heart. They need a new spirit. They have a bad heart that leads them to sin. They have a weak spirit that prevents them from rising to greatness. But that's okay. I'm going to do something about it. What they can't do for themselves, I'm going to accomplish.' We had a problem. But the Father guaranteed provision!

Chapter 3 – PROVISION

Ezekiel 36: 26-27

"I will give you a new heart and put a new spirit in you; I will remove from you your heart of stone and give you a heart of flesh. And I will put my Spirit in you and move you to follow my decrees and be careful to keep my laws." (New International Version)

All Mankind had a problem. The Bible makes it clear what that problem is. We have an unholy nature. Our heart, our will, is not intent upon pleasing God. In fact, the human will leads us away from God into different paths of evil. It's not merely that at times we commit acts of disobedience. The reality is that we ARE disobedient! Worse still is the fact that we are powerless to do anything to change the situation. We are slaves to that old nature.

In writing to the church at Rome, Paul referred to the fact that they had at one time been "slaves of sin". As sinners and slaves to sin, our hearts were filled with and our lives covered over by the effects of sin. The prophet Isaiah described our plight with the following words of the Amplified Version.

Isaiah 64:6

"For we have all become like one who is unclean (ceremonially, like a leper), and all our righteousness (our best deeds of rightness and justice) is like filthy rags or a polluted garment."

We were born sinners that were slaves to sin. Our lives were clothed with the filthy rags of sin. We looked like slaves to sin.

But thanks be to God! He didn't create Mankind to be slaves to sin. And where we were helpless to do anything about our situation, He stepped in! We were powerless, but our Father stepped in to make provision.

Through His servant Ezekiel, God promised His people the hope of three transformations in their lives. First, He promised that He was going to give them a new heart. God knew that as long as His people continued to have a heart for sin they would always go back to it. They needed a new heart.

Secondly, He promised that He was going to put a new spirit within them. Not only was He going to give them a new desire, He was going to put within them the power to do the right things. I believe that this is exactly what Paul was speaking of when we consider the following passage from the Amplified Version.

Philippians 2:13
"[Not in your own strength] for it is God who is all the while effectually at work in you [energizing and creating in you the power and desire], both to will and to work for His good pleasure and satisfaction and delight."

It certainly seems that Paul was in essence saying, 'Not only will God cause you to want to do the things that please Him, furthermore He will actually work through you to help you do these things!'

The third promise that God made to His people seems to confirm the accuracy of this reality.

Ezekiel 36:27
"And I will put my Spirit within you and cause you to walk in My statutes, and you shall heed My ordinances and do them."

God was saying with the help of my Spirit I'm going to enable you to walk in obedience to my ways. God spoke to people that were thoroughly unable to live lives of obedience and told them that He was going to help them to be obedient.

He promised that He would make this become reality. How? By the Provision that He planned for them.

Joel 2:28-29
"And it shall come to pass afterward, that I will pour out my Spirit upon all Flesh; and your sons and daughters shall prophecy, your old men shall dream dreams, your young men shall see visions: And also upon the servants and the handmaids in those days will I pour out my Spirit."

Let's examine that passage closely. Joel said that "it shall come to pass 'afterward'." After what? Paul helps us to understand this issue with these words:

Galatians 4:3-5
"Even so we, when we were children, were in bondage under the elements of the world:

But when the fullness of time was come, God set forth his Son, made of a woman, made under the law

To redeem them that were under the law that we might receive the adoption of sons."

According to Paul, we were in bondage. Then God sent His Son Jesus to redeem all Mankind from our sin.

When we were yet sinners, our lives were covered by the filthiness, the unrighteousness of sin.

Then Jesus came that He might pay the price to redeem us from our slavery to sin. Paul told Timothy in I Timothy 2:6 that Jesus "gave Himself as a ransom for all". John tells us in I John 4:10 that "He loved us and sent His Son to be the propitiation (the atoning sacrifice) for our sins". (Amplified Version)

When Jesus gave his life to redeem us, or pay the price for our sins, He didn't buy us in order to make us "slaves to righteousness".

John 15:15

"I no longer call you servants, because a servant does not know his master's business. Instead, I have called you friends, for everything that I learned from my Father I have made known to you." (New International Version)

Jesus didn't buy us to make us servants. He came to call us His friends. But there's more to this calling than just friendship.

John 1:12

"But as many as received him, to them gave He power to become the sons of God, even to them that believe on his name:" (King James Version)

Jesus came to do more than free us from sin. He came to do more than just grant us friendship with God. He came to give us the Power to become the Sons of God.

Romans 8:15

"The Spirit you received does not make you slaves, so that you live in fear again; rather, the Spirit you received brought about your adoption to sonship. And by him we cry, 'Abba, Father'."

Here Paul is speaking of the heart of men. I believe that he is referring to that 'heart change' that Ezekiel spoke of. He assures us that if we have accepted Jesus, we do not have to fear any longer. He tells us that we have "received" the spirit of adoption. This word received, used in this passage, comes from the same root of the Greek word that is found in John 20:22. In this passage, Jesus instructed his disciples to "Receive the Holy Ghost". When the Holy Spirit comes into the life of a believer, they can rest assured that they are no longer a slave but have become a Son of God.

Our Father has made provision for us to be victorious and overcome the sin problem that plagues our species.

As Ezekiel prophesied, God did a miraculous work to give us a "new heart". And He did something supernatural to ensure that we would have a "new spirit" within us.

He sent the Holy Spirit to "fill" our lives and dwell within us. In John 14:17, Jesus spoke of the Holy Spirit. He told His disciples that the Holy Spirit would not only "be" with them, but that, in fact, He would "dwell" in them. Jesus assured His disciples that the coming of the Holy Spirit would also bring great manifestation of supernatural power INTO their lives.

Not only did the Holy Spirit come to fill their inward beings with power, He came to do an outward work as well.

Luke 24:49

"And, behold, I send the promise of my Father upon you: but tarry ye in the city of Jerusalem, until ye be endued with power from on high." (King James Version)

Chapter 3 – Provision

When Jesus gave these instructions to His disciples, it was prior to His departure. It was prior to Pentecost. As Jesus looked upon His disciples, He saw people that had been freed from sin. But I believe that He also saw people that needed a Holy Ghost makeover if they were going to stay free from sin. They needed to be "dressed for success" in the spiritual realm.

When He told them to return to Jerusalem, they were told to wait until, in the King James language, they were "endued with power from on high". In the original Greek, the word endued has at least two meanings that we should consider. First, it can mean "to invest with clothing". Let's think of that in these terms: When you join the military, you are presented with a uniform, and you are expected to put it on and wear it! Our God has invested into our spiritual well-being by pouring out His Holy Spirit. He expects His soldiers to get in line and get their uniform. Secondly, the word "endued" can mean "to have put on". We can draw from this the idea of someone helping us to get properly dressed. Our Father has not only made available to us the covering or clothing of the Holy Spirit, but He has said if you will just come to me, I will help you 'put on' that clothing.

Everything we need has been provided for us to live obedient, overcoming lives. The Father has provided it.

Provision awaited the first disciples. All that they had to do was be obedient and step into PENTECOST.

Chapter 4 – PENTECOST

Acts 1:5, 8
"but ye shall be baptized with the Holy Ghost not many days hence…. But ye shall receive power, after that the Holy Ghost is come upon you."

At the exact moment the Holy Spirit of God fell upon and filled each of the 120 believers gathered in the upper room. They all began to speak in other tongues as the Spirit gave them the utterance. This was the initial physical outward indication of their experience. It was a vital element of their experience. And it would be seen again and again as others experienced their own baptism of the Holy Ghost. Yet this experience of being filled and speaking with tongues was neither the sum total of nor the end of their experience.

Jesus had told them that when the Holy Ghost came upon them they would receive power and they would 'be' witnesses. The record that we have, that's commonly known as the Acts of the Apostles, is the presentation to us of how the Holy Spirit empowered believers to change their world. It has been said more than once that the Book of Acts should have been called the Acts of the Holy Spirit, for it was the Spirit of Christ operating through yielded lives that accomplished such great works.

When the Holy Spirit fell upon the believers, His first work was to perform a work in the disciples' hearts. An examination of the days immediately prior to the Day of Pentecost reveals to us that the last time the disciples, as a collective group, were faced by an angry crowd and possible conflict that their reaction was much less than courageous. It was in fact a moment when they were all a bunch of cowards!

Mark 14:50

"And they all forsook him and fled."

Chapter 4 – Pentecost

These were individuals whose natural hearts were filled with fear. Of themselves they were not cut out to be people of great character, much less messengers and ministers of the Kingdom. But that was okay. It wasn't meant for them to exist and function for God in the power of their own might. That's why the Holy Spirit came.

When the Spirit of God came upon these disciples, something supernatural occurred. In an instant they went from being filled with cowardice to being courageous. They were no longer denying Jesus. Instead, they were declaring Jesus to be Lord. They were no longer seeking somewhere to hide from danger. Rather, they were taking to the streets to present the Gospel.

Much more than just experiencing the phenomenon of speaking in other tongues, Pentecost was the Divine in-pouring of God into the lives of natural people to change their nature and make them strong through God. The Apostle Paul got the clear revelation of this and expressed it in this passage:

II Corinthians 12:9
"But he said to me, 'My grace is sufficient for you, for my power is made perfect in

weakness.' Therefore I will boast all the more gladly about my weaknesses, so that Christ's power may rest on me." (NIV)

This is part of what makes God's dealings with men so incredible. He is not looking for polished, prepared professionals that of themselves can do great things for the Kingdom of God. Rather, He is looking for faulted, flesh and blood that recognizes our own weakness yet will dare to submit to His power to change us and produce change in our world. Someone has made the appropriate statement that God does not call the 'enabled', but rather that He enables the 'called'.

This was what happened on the day of Pentecost. Men that were virtually afraid to be seen in public, thereafter came and went from the Temple with reckless abandon. When called in before the Jewish religious leaders (Acts 4:15-21), Peter and John stood with complete boldness and declared the message of Jesus as Messiah. They had been filled with the Holy Ghost. They were changed.

The same Holy Spirit worked mightily in the lives of two men named Paul and Silas. Because their bold testimony of Jesus upset the local citizens, they were beaten, put in jail and locked away in the inner prison with their feet bound by stocks. Average men would have given up in the midst of this difficult situation. But Paul and Silas were not average men. They were men that had been touched and changed by the work of the Power of the Holy Spirit. During the darkest time of the night, they began to pray and sing praises to God. Something rising up out of their hearts reached beyond that dungeon to touch the heart of the One that sits upon Heaven's throne. Suddenly, the Power of God shook that jail, and the captives were set free! Because two men were willing to glorify God in the midst of their wounds and weaknesses, numerous souls came into the Kingdom that night.

The Holy Spirit came to change, to transform, natural people into supernatural representatives of the Kingdom of God.

The Holy Spirit came to cause the words of mere men to become the power packed words of God. As we have already referred to in Acts 4:13, the religious leaders were amazed that unlearned, ignorant men could be so knowledgeable and authoritative with the Word of God.

We have to understand the following facts: First, the original believers did not have the benefit of the New Testament writings that we have. We read the stories, but they lived them! Secondly, for the most part, they probably had very limited access to the Old Testament writings because those writings were held by the religious leaders at the time. Thirdly, these people had very limited educational opportunities in that era. So these men were neither educated nor eloquent when it was time to present their witness. Yet there was something, more so SOMEONE, that was with them. He was giving them every word that they were to say.

Matthew 10:19-20

"But when they deliver you up, take no thought how or what ye shall speak. For it shall be given you in that same hour what ye shall speak, for it is not ye that speak but the Spirit of your Father which speaketh in you."

Chapter 4 – Pentecost

These men had more than an education could provide them. They were filled with the Spirit who is the very Creator of all knowledge. Because they had the very source of all information dwelling in them, they had instant access, immediate revelation as they depended upon Him.

John 16:13

"Howbeit when he, the Spirit of truth, is come, he will guide you into all the truth: for he shall not speak of himself: but whatsoever he shall hear, that shall he speak: and he will show you things to come."

Because of the Holy Spirit's presence in their lives, their words were packed with a power that penetrated people's hardened hearts.

Acts 2:37

"Now when they heard this they were stung (cut) to the heart and they said to Peter and the rest of the apostles (special messengers) Brethren, what shall we do?" (AV)

People that have not experienced the Grace of God, despite what society may believe, do not merely need re-education. They need transformation. This happens only when the Gospel of Jesus Christ is presented in the Power of the Holy Spirit. When Heaven confronts people with the Truth, then comes conviction.

John 16:8
"And when he is come, he will reprove the world of sin, and of righteousness, and of judgment."

The Holy Spirit came to not only present a message that penetrated people's hearts; He came to produce a conviction that would draw them to repentance.

Real Pentecost is the Power of God changing His people's nature to the supernatural. It is the Power of God causing their communication to be Truth anointed with conviction.

The Holy Spirit came upon those first believers to flow through them in order to meet the needs of the masses. After reading in Acts Chapter two regarding the outpouring of Pentecost, immediately we read of a healing miracle in the following chapter.

Chapter 4 – Pentecost

There was a lame man that for a long time had sat at the gate called Beautiful begging for alms. This man needed to know Jesus as His Savior. But he also needed help for his immediate condition. He needed a miracle. And because they were filled with the power of the Holy Spirit, Peter grabbed the man's hand and jerked him up out of his crippled condition in the name of Jesus. The man got his miracle. A crowd gathered almost instantly, and Peter presented them with the message of repentance in the name of Jesus.

Acts 5:12
"And by the hands of the apostles were many signs and wonders wrought among the people."

The Holy Spirit came to demonstrate the love of God by healing and helping hopeless, hurting people. He came to flow through people who would be willing vessels that He might manifest through. The disciples understood this. They operated in this power. The Bible makes it evident that healings and miracles were so common at that time that people would place their sick in the streets hoping that

Peter's shadow might come upon them when they passed by – Acts 5:15.

Throughout the Book of Acts, from the beginning to the end, there are records and stories of miraculous healings. There's good reason for this. The Holy Spirit is the Spirit of Christ. Hebrews 13:8 tells us that He is the same yesterday, today, and forever. We are still called to "be witnesses". We still have the mission of touching our world for Christ. The Holy Spirit is still the Spirit of Pentecost. He desires to fill our lives and change us. He desires to communicate through us the message of the Kingdom with power and conviction. And he desires to miraculously meet people's needs. He is the Power of Pentecost!

Chapter 5 – Present

II Timothy 3:1
"This know also, that in the last days perilous times shall come."

In the previous chapter, we examined the Church of the 1st century. We considered the effects of the power of the Holy Spirit with respect to the men, their message, and the miraculous. We saw the evidence of the Holy Spirit being very active in their lives.

Now it's time to fast forward to the 21st century. It's time to be honest and give consideration to the condition of the Church in this hour.

Paul told Timothy to "know" this. The Amplified Version presents it as "But understand this". The word "know" in the original Greek has numerous possible meanings that can be applicable in this passage of Scripture. Among them is the meaning "be aware of", which could also be stated "beware of". I believe that Paul was not only saying "be aware of" what is happening, he was further saying 'don't get caught up in it'.

Paul said, "**Be aware** that in the last days perilous times shall come."

The Amplified Version says it this way:

II Timothy 3:1
"But understand this, that in the last days will come (set in) perilous times of great stress and trouble (hard to deal with and hard to bear)."

Paul tells his readers that times of great stress and great difficulty will set in during the last days. He then begins to describe the character, or rather the lack of character, that would be exhibited among the people of the last days. Let's look at this from the Amplified Version.

Chapter 4 – Pentecost

> II Timothy 3:2
> *"For people will be lovers of self and (utterly) self-centered, lovers of money and aroused by an inordinate (greedy) desire for wealth, proud and arrogant and contemptuous boasters. They will be abusive (blasphemous, scoffing), disobedient to parents, unholy, and profane."*

Paul tells us that in the last days "self" was going to be exalted. Has there ever been a more me-centered generation than at this present time? Have there ever been more people that believe they are entitled to life's best simply because they are alive and breathing?

Further, we are told that people would be aroused by greed and would be proud and arrogant. Do we not see this all around us in this hour? Paul goes on to add that they would be scoffers, disobedient to parents/ authority, ungrateful, unholy, and profane. Is this not a clear description of this modern society in which we live? People all around us act as if things are always going to go on as they are. There is no need to pay attention to any warnings of soon coming judgment. The media encourages society to cast off "outdated" morality and embrace a new lifestyle of "freedom". Much of secular higher education encourages students to question their parents' values and views. All around us those lifestyles that were once considered conservative and righteous are being rejected as religious and restrictive. The media venues are a continuous flow of communications that once would never have been allowed by the Federal Communications Commission.

In verses 3 and 4 of this chapter, Paul went on describing the character of people in the last days.

II Timothy 3:4b
"[They will be] lovers of sensual pleasures and vain amusements more than any other than lovers of God."

This King James Version offers us this:

II Timothy 3:4b
"lovers of pleasures more than lovers of God;"

Is it possible that there has ever been an era in which pleasure has been more pursued by society than today? People are consumed with not just a trip to the beach, but a condo to stay in. Getting to attend a ballgame isn't enough. They want a furnished skybox to watch it from. This modern society of ours is consumed with pleasure and entertainment.

But here is where it gets scary. These people that Paul speaks of love their pleasure, and they think that they love God too. It's not that they don't want some measured form of relationship with God. It's just that they want to love the things of this world as much as they love God. In the last days there will be people that don't truly understand what John meant in the following verse:

I John 2:15
"Love not the world, neither the things that are in the world. If any man loves the world, the love of the Father is not in him."

The most frightening fact concerning these people is presented to us at this point:

II Timothy 3:5
"Having a form of godliness, but denying the power thereof: from such turn away."

In II Timothy 3:1-4 Paul was **not** speaking of the people outside of the Church. In fact, he was describing the condition of THE CHURCH. He said that in the last days, people would have a form of godliness. They would have their religious activities and events. But they would reject the power of God from having an effect on their character. Let us consider how the Amplified Version presents this to us:

II Timothy 3:5

"[T]hey deny and reject and are strangers to the power of it (their conduct belies the genuineness of their profession)."

In essence, Paul seems to be saying, 'They will claim that they are Christians but their conduct and their character will show that actually they have rejected the Holy Spirit's efforts to change them into the character of Christ.'

Let's compare the past with the present. In the 1st century Church when the Holy Spirit came, the disciples' characters were changed. Liars lied no more. Cowards became courageous. Their lives and lifestyles were changed as the Power of Heaven remade them into the People of God. What does the modern American-European church look like for the most part today? Divorce, which is something that God hates (see Malachi 2:16 – It's still in the Book!), is commonplace among Christians. Sexual immorality, pornography, and lust reaches from the pews to the pulpits. Many that claim to be His people spend much more time loving this world than they do loving and pursuing the things of God. They don't deny God. They just aren't open to the Holy Spirit taking the world out of their hearts. They want no part of the Holy Spirit attempting to truly change them.

We've considered the men of then and now. At this point, let's consider the Holy Spirit and the message of the Church then and now.

The Book of Acts presents us with the picture of the 1st century Church's message. From the first message preached on the day of Pentecost until the closing verse of Acts, Chapter 28, the message remained the same. The focus was always upon addressing the prophecies of the Old Testament and presenting how Jesus of Nazareth had fulfilled all these prophecies. That is, He is the source of salvation for all Mankind. Their message was clear. Furthermore, it was confrontational:

Acts 4:12

"Neither is there salvation in any other: for there is no other name under heaven given among men, whereby we must be saved."

They made no attempt whatsoever to present Christ in such a way as to convince society to readily accept them and give them a place in the "religious" arena. They confronted people boldly with the truth that Jesus is the only way anyone can enter the Father's Family.

Their message was encouraging. But it was not a message of ease or entertainment.

Acts 14:22

"Confirming the souls of the disciples, and exhorting them to continue in the faith, and that we must through much tribulation enter into the Kingdom of God."

Let's consider the Amplified Version here.

Acts 14:22

"and [telling them] that it is through many hardships and tribulations we must enter the Kingdom of God."

The first disciples didn't spend their time educating the ignorant masses concerning all the benefits that could be had through faith in Jesus. They did not focus their efforts upon the message of prosperity as an indication of God's blessings.

Consider with me the testimony of one of the primary figures presented to us in the Book of Acts. Let's consider what Paul had to say about the message that he preached to people.

I Corinthians 1:23

"But we preach Christ crucified."

Paul's message was centrally focused upon the Good News offered to Mankind through the Life, Death, and Resurrection of Jesus. He understood that in order to present a resurrected redeemer, there first had to have been a crucified lamb.

The message of the 1st century was this: confession of Jesus as Messiah, followed by a faith walk that involved denying one's self-will and following after the teachings of Jesus Christ. It was a message that believers were to be filled with the Holy Spirit and be led by Him. This was to result in people giving up themselves so that Christ might live through them.

Galatians 2:20
"I am crucified with Christ: nevertheless I live; yet not I, but Christ liveth in me: and the life which I now live in the flesh I live by the faith of the Son of God, who loved me, and gave himself for me."

Finally, in contemplating the message of the 1st century church, let's consider this: When the messengers of God preached and presented Christ to their audiences, the messages were charged with conviction. There was power that went forth with every word they spoke. This power convicted the hearts of them that were ready for repentance. And it chastened or rebuked the hearts of the religious and rebellious. The message that they preached always had an effect upon its audience.

Let's compare the message of then with that of today. How often do preachers confront people with the message that Jesus is the only way to the Father? When is the last time you heard an old fashioned message on holiness and the need for repentance? How many ministries are preaching the Cross, the Power of the Blood, and a lifestyle of truly following Christ and surrendering one's self to Him? Do you recall the last time that you heard a message on the soon return of Jesus for His Church? These are subjects that aren't too popular in much of the Church today. I suspect that many preachers want to pack a pew and pad the offering plates. They desire to present speeches that will "inspire" the people to return and hear them again. But here's the question that needs to be asked: Are these messages really leading people to the Jesus of Revelation, Chapter 1:13-17? Is the message of today's Church the message that will truly introduce people to the One that wants to be their Lord? Is the message that is going out from many pulpits "Go with God"? Do the words have ANY power upon them, much less enough power to grip people's hearts to draw them to an altar of repentance? How many messages are more like a take-it or leave-it buffet rather than a fiery fresh word from Heaven that stirs people to desire what they truly need? How frequently do services occur where people never experience the least bit of conviction coming upon them during the preaching of the Gospel?

What was the message of then? The message of Christ, the cross, and the requirement to repent. What is today's message? All too often, at best, it is a vague, veiled effort to connect people with Jesus without commanding that they must forsake evil and follow Him. At worst, it is informative, inspirational, motivational speeches designed to encourage people and make them feel like they are a part of something good.

Lastly, having considered the effects of the Holy Spirit upon the men and the messages of then and now, let us consider the miracles of the first Church.

The following witness is offered to us:

Mark 16:20
"And they went forth and preached everywhere, the Lord working with them and confirming the word with signs following. Amen."

Additionally, we are provided this insight:

Acts 5:12
"And by the hands of the apostles were many signs and wonders wrought among the people."

The people of the 1st century Church were a people that walked in the ministry of the miraculous. Their words went forth with conviction. They declared life over people. Lame people started walking. Blind people started seeing. Demons were cast out. The dead were brought back to life. They were a people that understood that not only COULD God supernaturally work in lives, but that He WANTED to work in people's lives. These Christians, the Servants of the Lord, lived their lives looking for opportunities for God to demonstrate His power. When Paul wrote the first letter to the church of Corinth, he reminded them of the following:

I Corinthians 2:4
"And my speech and my preaching was not with enticing words of man's wisdom but in demonstration of the Spirit and of power."

It seems that Paul said, "I didn't just come to you with words alone. No, I demonstrated the Power of the Spirit." This is additionally established by the following words:

Acts 19:11
"And God wrought special miracles by the hands of Paul.""

The audiences that were exposed to the 1st century preachers of the Gospel experienced more than a ministry of words. They witnessed with their eyes the Power of God working through His disciples to set people free from all sorts of evil. They saw firsthand the expressed Love of God healing people of their diseases. The 1st century church walked in close fellowship with the presence of God, and the signs and evidence of the supernatural followed them.

How does that compare to now? Today? Here in America? The Western Church? In many church organizations they haven't seen the supernatural in so long that they don't even expect it anymore. In fact, many have gone to great lengths to explain away the absence of the Awesome in their church. Others, while claiming they believe, are not experiencing the manifest miraculous. Why? Perhaps it is because they have come to believe that God in His "Sovereignty" does not will to move. That is to say, that God no longer performs miracles.

It is true that God is Sovereign. Furthermore, it is plainly evident that Jesus did not heal everybody, every single place that He went. Yet nowhere in the Book of Acts do we see the disciples seeking the will of God nor praying prayers to the effect of "If it is Your will, Lord." No. Jesus told them they would receive power. They did. Jesus told them: Heal the sick, raise the dead, preach, present the Kingdom. They did. And because they were obedient, Heaven moved to confirm the Word with the miraculous.

Much of today's American church is mired in the misery of that awful place that is the absence of the Awesomeness of God. Nothing supernatural is happening. Why? Because nobody expects, believes, or longs for it to happen. People are being educated and informed about biblical principles. But nobody is being delivered or healed because the Power is not manifest. This is the sad condition of much of the modern church. They have not because they ask not.

We close out this chapter with this consideration:

Acts 1:11

"'Men of Galilee,' they said, 'why do you stand here looking into the sky? This same Jesus, now has been taken from you into heaven, will come back in the same way you have seen him go into heaven." (NIV)

If this same Jesus is coming back, do you think, perhaps, that maybe, just maybe, He expects to return for the same kind of Church that He established in the 1st century? If this is in fact the case, than we, in our present condition, are in desperate need to again examine and experience the Promise that Heaven has offered us.

Chapter 6 – THE PROMISE

Acts 2:16-17
"But this is that which was spoken by the prophet Joel; And it shall come to pass in the last days, saith God, I will pour out my Spirit upon all flesh:"

At this point, let's reflect upon this passage of scripture. It was the Day of Pentecost. The believers who gathered together in the upper room had just experienced for themselves the outpouring of the Holy Spirit. They had been baptized in the Holy Ghost and fire, even as John the Baptist had foretold would happen.

When faced with an immediate need to explain this to the curious crowd that had assembled, without hesitancy, Peter referred them to the prophecy that had been given by Joel regarding the outpouring of God's Holy Spirit. Peter authoritatively told those gathered: This is THAT PROMISE.

Additionally, under the influence of the Holy Spirit, Peter declared that God had said, "And it shall come to pass in the last days." With that proclamation, Peter asserted that the last days' timeframe had begun.

In all likeliness none of the church leaders of that hour would have guessed that more than 2,000 years would pass without the return of Jesus Christ. Yet here we are today. Many might say that Peter did not have a clue when he declared that the "last days" had begun. This attitude is all around us today. It is an attitude of disbelief. It is a rejection of the Biblical message that time will surely have a sudden confrontation with the God of Eternity. These people do not realize nor accept that they themselves are a sign of the times that we are living in.

II Peter 3:3-4

"Knowing this first, that there shall come in the last days scoffers, walking after their own lusts, And saying, Where is the promise

Chapter 6 – The Promise

of his coming? For since the fathers fell asleep, all things continue as they were from the beginning of the creation."

People like this do not understand that the Eternal God is not operating on man's timetable. He is acting in accordance with His Plan. And He is acting in mercy in fulfilling His Plan. But as Peter reminds us in verse 9 of that same chapter: "The Lord is not slack concerning his promise."

Mankind is living in the last days, even the last hours of what we call the 'church age'. Biblical prophecies are being fulfilled at an alarming rate. The question is: Is anybody paying attention to the alarm?

If the last days began on the Day of Pentecost, does not logic cause us to reason that with all these prophecies being brought to pass, surely we are in the last hours and moments?

Let us consider another prophecy that is most certainly being fulfilled in this hour that we live in. This prophecy is found in another Bible passage regarding the last days.

Matthew 24:12

"And because iniquity shall abound, the love of many shall wax cold."

Let's also consider that scripture from the Amplified Version.

Matthew 24:12

"And the love of the great body of people will grow cold because of the multiplied lawlessness and iniquity."

In speaking to His audience concerning the end times, Jesus declared that iniquity shall abound. That word iniquity has its origin in the Greek word anomia. It can mean the following: illegality, violation of law, wickedness.

Jesus described the last days as being a time of great wickedness. He said that people would be lawbreakers, violators of society's laws. Further he said that this "iniquity" would abound. The word "abound" in its original Greek can mean 'to increase'. It can even mean 'to multiply'.

Are we not seeing such behavior all around us in this hour we live? Many laws are looked upon as suggestions and treated with contempt. Society more and more has given place to situational ethics in replacement of the values and morality of those who preceded us. Truly we are living in an hour that is a fulfillment of the following passage of scripture:

> Proverbs 29:18a
> *"Where there is no revelation,
> people cast off restraint;"*

In this hour that we are living in, there are many people that want the authorities to protect them from being hurt but not prevent them from the activities that expose them to being harmed. They do not want restraints or laws placed upon them. And in the middle of it all, a lovelessness is gripping our society.

Jesus said that in the midst of all this lawlessness that the love of many would grow cold. Perhaps he was speaking of the Church. But when we look at the world, we see an explosion of lovelessness all around us. Males fathering babies yet having no heart to be a father. Women left alone, choosing abortion as their only option for dealing with an unwanted pregnancy. Coldness has gripped the heart of our society.

These are all signs that were foretold of long ago. It is not God's pleasure that they are happening. But it was promised. It was foretold that this was going to be the condition of the last days.

But thank God that's not the only promise that we have to consider!

Romans 5:20
"But where sin abounded, grace did much more abound"

The Apostle Paul told his readers that where sin had increased, or multiplied, that God's grace had much more increased or abounded to Mankind.

He was speaking of how in the midst of a world of sin, that God had injected grace through Jesus Christ to rescue Mankind.

But when we read the Scriptures, we must understand that many time prophecies that were given were done with the intent that there would be more than one, even multiple fulfillments of them.

Chapter 6 – The Promise

I believe that we can consider Romans 5:20 in that light. Do we not live in an hour where sin is exploding all around us? Well, in order for God's Word to be accurate, where sin is being multiplied, is God not surely going to pour out His overcoming grace in the midst of it?

Paul said that God would cause grace to "much more abound". Now in the original Greek, the word for that phrase is highly important. It conveys to the reader the idea of super-abounding. That is to say, to exceed and to have more than enough. Paul said that in the middle of great difficulties that God was going to give His people Greater Grace.

It was this greatness that John referred to in the following passage:

I John 4:4
"Ye are of God, little children, and have overcome them: because greater is he that is in you than he that is in the world."

Now there's a promise that we can take a hold of! John tells us that "He" that is in us is greater than the "he" that is in this world. Sin may explode around us. That's okay. It's going to happen. We are in the end times. God's Grace, His Holy Spirit, has come to be with us and in us. He is the Greater One, and He has come to overcome the world for us and through us. The Holy Spirit is referred to in Hebrews 10:29 as the "Spirit of grace". He is the One that has come to help the Church testify of Jesus.

Sin is going to multiply, and evil will become more prevalent. What is to become of the Church of Jesus Christ? Will she cave in to compromise, wither away in weakness, and fade from the face of society? Not if the Holy Spirit has anything to say and do about it!

Ephesians 5:27
"That he might present it to himself a glorious church."

The Lord Jesus is going to come back to a "Glorious" Church. Not a sin-battered, beaten, compromised Church. He will return for a people that are victorious in their struggle against evil.

II Corinthians 2:14
"Now thanks be to God, which always causeth us to triumph in Christ."

Chapter 6 – The Promise

We are assured that in these last days, we will be the overcomers.

Romans 8:37
"No, in all these things we are more than conquerors through him who loved us." (NIV)

We have been promised that we will overcome this world. We will be more than conquerors because the One that is Greater lives within us. These are all promises that we have to hold onto in these evil hours.

The last Promise that I want us to consider is this:

Haggai 2:9
"The glory of this latter house shall be greater than of the former, saith the Lord of hosts."

The Prophet Haggai was talking about the physical Temple of the Jews. This prophecy was fulfilled once, long ago when the Jewish Temple was first rebuilt. The Jews were focused upon providing a place for the Presence of God to abide in. In these times, however, thanks to our having the entire Bible available to us, we can understand that Man has never built a house that can truly contain the glory of God. Solomon testified of this in the following scripture:

I Kings 8:27

"But will God indeed dwell on the earth? behold the heaven and heaven of heavens cannot contain thee: how much less this house that I have built?"

No earthly hands have ever built a house that the glory of God truly "dwells in". Yet there is a dwelling place which the Almighty God Himself has designed for the purpose of living in.

I Corinthians 3:16

"Know ye not that ye are the Temple of God and that the Spirit of God dwelleth in you?"

Let's consider that verse in the Amplified Version.

"Do you not discern and understand that you [the whole church at Corinth] are God's temple (His sanctuary), and that God's Spirit has His permanent dwelling in you [to be

at home in you, collectively as a church and also individually]?"

I like that! I believe Paul was saying, 'Do you not understand that collectively as the People of God we are His Temple; yet, individually we are His Temple as well?' In other words, when we all come together, we are His people; and His Glory will dwell among us. Yet when we are all by ourselves, we are still His; and He wants to dwell in us.

We were made by God Himself to be a Living House that His Spirit can dwell in.

Ephesians 2:10
"For we are His workmanship."

We are all uniquely designed by the Hand of the Almighty Creator. We have been created for the purpose of being a 'house' for God.

Ephesians 2:22
"And in him you too are being built together to become a dwelling in which God lives by his Spirit." (NIV)

And just as surely as Esther of the Old Testament, we have been placed in this life for "such a time as this", Esther 4:14.

Jesus is coming back for His people. He is going to come back to His Temple one more time. And He will not come back to a rundown, worthless house. God is going to pour out His glory one more time! His Presence is going to come upon His People, His Temple, once again. And the latter condition of His Church is going to be greater than the condition of the former Church. Jesus will come back to and for that Church spoken of as a glorious, vibrant, victorious, overcoming Church.

Jesus, the Heavenly Bride-Groom, is coming back. He has promised. Heaven help us to be the Church, the bride that recognizes the soon return of her Groom and rises to prepare herself.

Chapter 7 – PREPARATION

Matthew 25:13
*"Watch therefore, for ye know neither the
day nor the hour wherein the
Son of man cometh."*

These words of Jesus came at the conclusion of a very important parable that He shared with His listeners. It is the parable of the ten virgins that had been invited to be part of a wedding party. The fact that this parable came at the latter part of Jesus' teaching concerning the end times is by no means a coincidence. Jesus shared with his audience the conditions of the end times and the grave difficulties that people were going to be facing. He then warned the people that they needed to be alert and not be caught unaware because the coming of the Son of

Man would be at an hour when most people were not looking for Him (Matthew 24:44). Then it would seem that Jesus turned his attention specifically to those that he would be returning for – His Church.

Jesus spoke of ten virgins who had lamps and how they all went out in order to meet the bridegroom. But the bridegroom delayed his coming, and the virgins had to wait for an uncertain amount of time. And although all these individuals were virgins, Jesus presented a distinguishing factor between these ten virgins. Five were considered wise, and five were counted as foolish. The distinguishing factor was not that some of them weren't virgins. They all were. It was not that five of them carried no lamps. They all did. It was not that half of them had never started out with the intent to meet the bridegroom. They all did. The only distinguishing factor that Jesus presented in this story is simply this: five of them carried a reserve, a supply of oil with them and five did not.

Now the purpose of addressing this passage is not to split theological hairs nor create controversy. But we must address this story as it relates to our issue. Oil has long been recognized as symbolic of the Holy Spirit. The Holy Spirit is the source of the

Chapter 7 – Preparation

very power or strength of God. So for our purposes, we are going to consider that Jesus was conveying a picture of 5 virgins that had a source of oil, strength, or energy so that when the critical hour came, they could prepare their lamps to go out and meet the bridegroom.

Sadly enough, this picture also presents the image of five believers, I mean virgins, that had no oil to prepare themselves in the hour that the bridegroom came.

They were all virgins. They all had lamps. They all heard the call. They all arose to put their lamps in order. But five weren't prepared. They had no oil, no energy. To put it plainly, they had no power.

I strongly believe that in presenting this story and following it with the admonition in verse 13, Jesus was warning his hearers that they needed to be sure to be prepared for His coming. He communicated to them that they didn't need to be like the five foolish virgins and neglect their need for oil, or strength, in order to be able to survive the delay and be prepared for the bridegroom's calling.

As we move closer and closer to the time of Jesus' return for His people, I believe that it is urgent that we understand our great need for proper preparation. We should consider the words of the Amplified Version:

Romans 13:11-12a

"Besides this you know what [a critical] hour this is, how it is high time now for you to wake up out of your sleep (rouse to reality). For salvation (final deliverance) is nearer to us now than when we first believed (adhered to, trusted in, and relied on Christ, the Messiah). The night is far gone and the day is almost here."

This is a critical hour. We are nearer to Christ's return than ever before. The night is far gone. That is to say that there is not much time left before Jesus comes back. We need to make preparations. What do I mean by preparations? What steps do we need to take?

First, we need to HEAR what the Spirit is saying to us, the Church. Throughout His earthly ministry, Jesus would often say, "He that has ears to hear, let him hear". Most all of us have ears. And unless there is an unnatural situation, we were blessed with two healthy ears for the purpose of being able to listen with them. Unfortunately, many times we're not really paying attention like we should. So the words may be spoken but they didn't really register with us. I believe Jesus was really saying, "This is important." Pay close attention. When Jesus addressed the seven churches of Asia in John's book of Revelation, He repeatedly said, "He that has ears to hear, let him hear what the Spirit is saying to the Church." We need to be giving close attention to the directions that our Lord is providing for us in these ever-increasingly evil times.

John 10:27
"My sheep hear my voice, and I know them and they follow me."

If we're going to follow Jesus into all that He has for us, it is vital that we are listening to hear what He is saying. We need to be HONEST about our situation.

Now for those that have bought into the teaching that the times of the Apostles was long ago or that since we now have the Bible that God simply no longer reveals Himself as He once did, well there's not much that I can really say other than, REALLY?

Hebrews 13:8
"Jesus Christ the same yesterday, and today and forever."

God hasn't died, and He hasn't changed. He was a God of miracles, divine revelations and supernatural manifestations in the Old Testament. He poured out signs and wonders in the 1st century Church. History is filled with records of miracles that have occurred for those who will honestly look for them. And in this modern hour, miracles, signs and wonders are happening in many places around the world, especially in places where people haven't been taught to doubt and disbelieve.

But let's be honest. What about in our nation? How about in our region? Our communities? Our church? How about in any and all of our lives? What are the signs, the indicators of the Power of God working in our lives? Do we live lives that are being purified and becoming more and more like the character of God? Do we have strong convictions that cause us to be consistent in our faith? Is there so much of the Presence of God in and upon our lives that others come under conviction and cry out for spiritual direction simply from coming in contact with us? Are our lives and words communicating a clear, confronting presentation that Jesus is the only name by which men may be saved and that all must repent or face the certainty of eternity apart from God? When is the last time that someone asked you to pray a prayer of faith for their loved one to be healed? When is the last time they laid their sick out on the sidewalk in hopes that our shadows might bring them miracles as we pass by?

Jesus is the same. He expects His Church to be the same. He is coming back for a Church that is overcoming, a victorious church and a Church that is walking in the Power that He has made available to us.

We need to be honest. In most cases, we are living far beneath the level that God had called us to. We may still sing that "there is power in the blood", but very few are living in the power of the Holy Spirit like the Book of Acts Church!

There is need for additional honesty. There are those that say they believe in the Power of God, but it isn't really evident in their lives. And it's probably not going to be evident any time soon because they've come to believe that when God "wills" He will pour out what they need. Allow me to address the issue of Gods will for people. In 2 Peter 3:9, we are told that it is not Gods will that any should perish but rather that all should come to eternal life. In 1 Thessalonians 4:3, we are told this is the will of God even your sanctification. And in Ephesians 5:18, believers are instructed to be filled with the Spirit. It is the will and purpose of God that men be saved, set apart from sin, and filled with His Holy Spirit. The only issue of will that we face is this: what will we believe and are we really willing to receive?

James 4:2

"[Y]e have not, because ye ask not."

Whenever Heaven has something for us, if we don't experience and receive it, it's not God's fault. The problem has its roots in us. It's up to us to discover what we need to do so that we can experience God's blessings. That is the honest fact.

If we're going to prepare ourselves, we must <u>HUMBLE</u> our souls. Pride and dignity are the enemies of the Glory of God. God will not give us all that we

Chapter 7 – Preparation

need so long as we refuse to recognize our need. If we act like we can go on as we are, trust me, we will. If we are more concerned with other's opinions of us, how our public image appears, than we will have to make it on our own.

James 4:6
"But He gives us more and more grace (power of the Holy Spirit, to meet this evil tendency and all others fully). That is why He says, God sets Himself against the proud and haughty, but gives grace [continually] to the lowly (those who are humble enough to receive it)." (AV)

I fear that all too often, both in our individual lives and our corporate times of worship, we have invited Heaven to come in a "measured manifestation". We want only as much of God's power as we are comfortable with and believe that we can control. We've been so afraid that emotional people might get "out of control" that we've never let God take control. As long as we are afraid of the potential for "wildfire", there will never be the opportunity for the True Fire to fall. As long as pride remains alive within us, God will never show His mighty power.

James 4:8a, 10
"Draw nigh to God, and he will draw nigh to you…. Humble yourselves in the sight of the Lord, and he shall lift you up."

We've been instructed to make drawing near to the presence of God our priority. We've been assured that if we come towards Him that He will move to meet us. But we've been warned that if we are going to approach Him, we need to HUMBLE OURSELVES.

The true act of humbling one's self involves being cleansed from unrighteousness and compromise. Here's what the Amplified Version of the following passage tells us:

Psalm 34:18
"The Lord is close to those who are of a broken heart and saves such as are crushed with sorrow for sin and are humbly and thoroughly penitent."

There is something about our humbling ourselves and becoming repentant over our weaknesses that draws Heaven near to us. When God sees His children choosing to become broken, when He hears us crying over our own shortcomings, it moves Him to come closer to us.

II Samuel 6 provides the story of David's second effort to bring up the Ark of the Covenant (which was the physical representation of His presence among His people). In this story, we read of how David humbled himself before both the people and God. Verse 14 tells of how David danced before the Lord with all his might. In case you weren't aware of it, David was a Jew. Furthermore, if you weren't aware of it, the Old Testament Jewish culture significantly incorporated dance into their worship. The Hebrew word, from which the English word dance comes from, has an interesting meaning. It can mean not only to dance in certain organized steps, but to whirl or spin energetically. David didn't just do a basic two-step dance. He was passionately dancing and spinning in worship of God for the return of the 'Glory' of God to Jerusalem.

But that wasn't the full extent of David's humbling process. According to the testimony in verse 20 of that same chapter, David had removed his fancy outer garments, and he danced publicly in such a state of clothing (or lack of), that it could bring shame to an individual of his status. His wife was ashamed of him, and she poured out her contempt on him. Isn't that what the religious world does towards those that desperately want to worship God until the Glory comes again? But David didn't care. In fact, he pretty much said, I have only begun to humble myself! That's the attitude it is going to take if we want to prepare ourselves for the Power that God wants to pour out on us again!

Next, if we're going to prepare ourselves, we must HUNGER and seek what He has for us.

Matthew 5:6
"Blessed are they which do hunger and thirst after righteousness: for they shall be filled."

Jesus said that when it comes to experiencing the deeper things of God, there is a price that has to be paid to gain the prize. If you want to be filled, you have to "do" some hungering. There is some development of desire, some training of the tastes that has to happen. Have you ever heard someone speak of teaching their children to develop a taste for a certain type of food? That's a picture of how it is with spiritual things. In the following passage, Jesus spoke concerning this spiritual reality.

Luke 5:38-39

"But new wine must be put into new bottles: and both are preserved. No man, also having drunk old wine straightway, desireth new: for he saith, 'The old is better'."

Here Jesus clearly presents that having a "taste" for the old things can easily prevent an individual from having a desire for the new things that God has for them.

Something has to give. Change must be worked in the life. The appetite must be addressed and altered. Listen to the words from the Amplified Version of this verse:

Proverbs 27:7

"He who is satiated [with sensual pleasures] loathes and treads underfoot a honeycomb, but to the hungry soul every bitter thing is sweet."

That is to say, a person that is already filled up with the things of this world will have no hunger, no desire to receive the things of God. But for the person that has taken the time to do without and to get hungry, than whatever God has for them is satisfying!

One of the great problems facing the Church in this hour is our lack of spiritual appetite. We've filled ourselves for so long on the things of this world that we aren't really hungry for the things of God. We treat the things of God like they are merely a dish on an all-you-can-eat buffet bar and we can pick and choose as our tastes dictate.

If we, the Church, collectively and individually are going to receive that which God has for us, we've got to develop a hunger for the things of God.

This may involve pushing away from the table that we've been feasting at and choosing to do without for a time. We used to refer to it as fasting. If we want Heaven to fill us, we must get our vessels, our lives, emptied out of all the fleshly, worldly, foolishness that we've been guilty of filling our lives with.

It's time to follow after David's example:

Chapter 7 – Preparation

> Psalm 63:1-2
> *"O God thou art my God: early will I seek thee: my soul thirsteth for thee, my flesh longeth for thee in a dry and thirsty land, where no water is: To see thy power and thy glory, so as I have seen thee in the sanctuary."*

In times of economic crises or at moments when our health is threatened, we find it easy to get serious about crying out for help. When will we realize that our greatest need is to truly hunger after God Himself? When will we realize that He only reveals more of Himself when we get serious and hungry for Him?

> Jeremiah 29:13
> *"And ye shall seek me, and find me, when ye shall search for me with all your heart."*

If we are going to experience the power of God in our lives, we will have to prepare ourselves by hungering to be filled.

We must HEAR. We must be HONEST. We must HUMBLE ourselves. We must HUNGER. Lastly, we must HOLD on until we receive. That is to say, we must be persistent until we receive all that we need.

Our Heavenly Father is the One that pours out His Power upon and into our lives. We have a role in this event as well. We are the vessel. It's up to us to position ourselves and patiently persist until we get what we need.

We need to be like Jacob when he wrestled with the Angel of the Lord.

Genesis 32:26
"And he said I will not let thee go, except thou bless me."

It is commonly agreed upon by many scholars that the Angel referred in this story was, in reality, an Old Testament manifestation of the Son of God in physical form. God came down and had an up-close encounter with Jacob. Jacob realized that something supernatural was going on. And he decided that he needed God to do something special in his life. He needed a 'blessing'. It was so vital that he grabbed hold of the goodness of God and said, "I will not let you go until you bless me!"

Chapter 7 – Preparation

This is the kind of persistence, the diligence that God is looking for from His people.

Hebrews 11:6
"[A]nd that He is a rewarder of them that diligently seek Him."

In this hour of minute rice, microwave meals, instant grits, and immediate gratification, we've lost the art of waiting upon God.

Recently, the Holy Spirit impressed this thought upon me, "Many of my people spend more time taking a relaxing shower than they do waiting for my presence, my Power to wash over their lives."

But it's always been like that. I Corinthians 15:6 reports that at least 500 disciples witnessed Jesus after the Resurrection. Many believe that this was the number of disciples that actually heard His last words and witnessed His Ascension. They heard Jesus tell them that their immediate priority was to 'wait' upon the promise of the Father. Yet after the passing of nine full days, when the Day of Pentecost arrived, there were only 120 people that continued to wait for what had been promised. Quite likely, many more than just the 120 had initially gathered to obey the Lord's instructions. But the demands of life and the exhaustion of their patience probably took its toll on some. So they left. Others may have become overwhelmed with the lack of anything happening. They grew bored. So the number dwindled as the days passed.

Don't ask me why, but we serve a God that is not beyond testing our endurance. Perhaps He does so to allow us time for self-examination and the opportunity to submit to change. Perhaps He does so to see who is willing to obey and patiently trust. But He is the God that said, "Ask and keep on asking, seek and keep on seeking." He is the "rewarder" of those that will keep holding on until Heaven moves.

If we will act upon the principles that have been laid out, we will have the experience of receiving what we need from God.

Our God is still a God of power and might. He still desires for His Church to be a people that are 'filled' with His mighty power. There is still mighty power that is available for each and every one of us today. His Power is available. It is up to each one of us to position and to make ourselves available to Him.

Chapter 7 – Preparation

Have you ever been at home and suddenly got thirsty for some water? What was the solution? You got up and went to where the cups were at and got yourself something to hold some water. Then you went to the sink where the faucet was and turned it on. Then you put the cup, the vessel under the source that was pouring water and you held it there until it was filled. We are the vessels that God wants to fill. He is the source of these Living Waters. He waits upon us to come to Him and allow Him to fill our lives with His Power. It is up to us to recognize the real manifestations of His Power and to refuse to live any longer without it. It is up to us to take Him at His word:

Isaiah 40:31
"But they that wait upon the Lord shall renew their strength."

Acts 1:8
"But ye shall receive power."

THERE IS POWER FOR YOU.

TODAY.